Microsoft®
SharePoint Server 2010

Deployment Book

Mahmoud Abouelhassan
2013

First Edition

SharePoint 2010 Deployment Book
First Edition

Table of Contents

Chapter1: Introduction

1-1 About the Author

The author worked in the information technology field more than 15 years.

He started as Technical support engineer in Internet Service Provider. Supported many Microsoft products like NT 4.0, MS Exchange 5.0 and 5.5, and MS Proxy 2.0,.. etc.

After that, he worked as a Network Administrator in a company which is market leader in the technology field.

He supported wide range of Microsoft and non-Microsoft products, MS SQL version 7.0 to version 2012, SharePoint version 2001 to version 2010, BMC Remedy from version 4.0 to version 7.6, and other business applications.

During these years of experience, SharePoint is major service introduced by the IT department to all company operations as the collaboration tool required of internal communication and document library that keep all documented assets inside it.

During these years of experience Mahmoud obtained many Microsoft certifications like MCSE and MCDBA, and other Certifications like ITIL and ISO 20000 Practitioner certifications.

Moreover the Master's degree in computer science from Middlesex and the thesis was in the E-Commerce field in addition to the Advanced Management diploma.

1-2 About this Book

This book will help you in deploying SharePoint 2010 on Windows 2008 R2 and SQL 2008 R2 as standalone installation.

This book includes screen shots with lite explanation for every installation step.

Also this book contains reference URLs for IT professionals already worked on documenting their experience online for how to deploy SharePoint 2010.

The book contains five chapters as follows:

1-3 Chapter1 Introduction:
This introduction gives the reader quick review about the author and other chapters.

1-4 Chapter2: Windows 2008 R2 Deployment
This chapter will help you for how to deploy windows 2008 R2 as a recommended Operating System for SharePoint 2010.

For those who are familiar with Windows 2008 R2 installation can skip this chapter or read it rapidly.

1-5 Chapter3: SQL 2008 R2 Deployment
SQL 2008 R2 is recommended for SharePoint 2010 deployment especially for those who are intending to create large document libraries and want to create scheduled jobs, Integration Services Packages and have advance knowledge in SQL and want to get benefit from hit.

However this won't prevent you from using SQL 2008 express for SharePoint 2010 deployment.

But this Book is assuming that you will install SQL 2008 R2.

For those have a strong knowledge in deploying SQL 2008 R2 can skip this chapter or read it rapidly.

1-6 Chapter4: SharePoint 2010 Deployment

This chapter includes the required steps by screen shoots for how to install Windows features, roles and roles services required by SharePoint 2010. Then explain the software prerequisites required before installing SharePoint 2010.

Then explain the Installation Steps and the configuration wizard to start using your new SharePoint 2010 server.

1-7 Chapter5: Troubleshooting

This Chapter contains some error message and guides you, if you faced one of them, to solve these errors.

1-8 References:

This section is very important as it helps me a lot in deploying SharePoint 2010, and introduces help for me to write this book. Special thanks for their authors.

Chapter2: Windows 2008 R2 deployment

2-1 Windows Deployment

To start deploying Windows 2008 R2 you will need to:

1- Prepare your windows CD/DVD
2- Get the License Key
3- Prepare suitable machine with 4 GB RAM and Dual Core processor

Now insert CD/DVD into your CD/DVD ROM and power on your machine and choose to boot from your CD/DVD device.

Windows Loader will start to extract the installation files.

Figure 2-1: Windows Loader

Then Choose the language needed to be installed and click next

Figure 2-2: Windows Language Option

Click install now

Figure 2-3: Install Windows

Type your License Key and click next

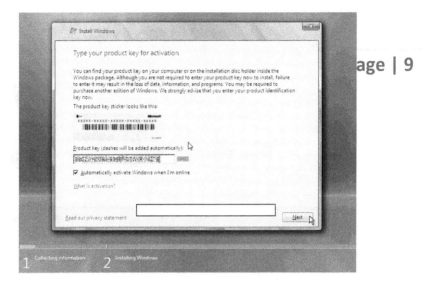

Figure 2-4: Windows License Key

Choose your licensed edition then click next

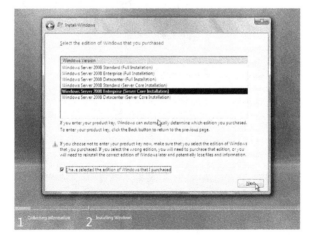

Figure 2-5: Windows Edition

Choose your Operating system then click next

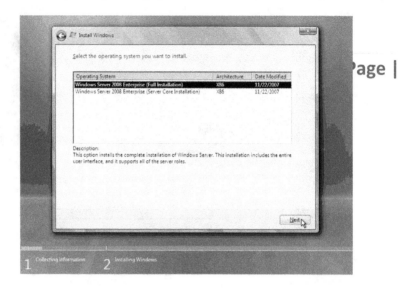

Figure 2-6: Operating System Selection

Read the License terms and mark on I accept the license terms to be able to continue and click next

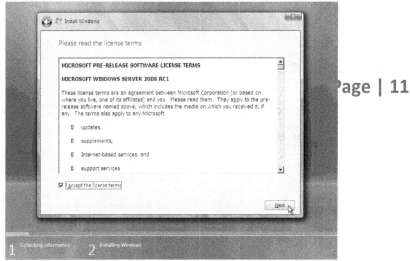

Figure 2-7: License Terms

Click on Custom (Advanced) option

Figure 2-8: Windows Installation

Click on the drive that you want to install windows on it and click next or click on Drive Options (advanced) if you want to re-partition of hard disk

Figure 2-9: Choose Drive

Windows installation wizard will start installing the operating system according to the above inputs

Figure 2-10: Windows Installation Progress

Now press CTRL, ALT and DELETE buttons on your computer keyboard to start using your new Windows operating system.

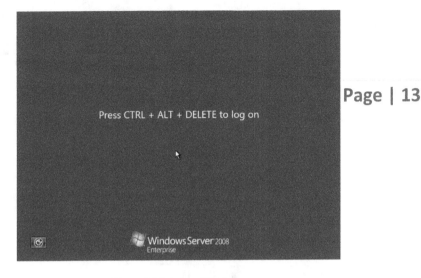

Figure 2-11: Logon Window

After installing Windows 2008 R2, you need to connect the new server to the network and configure its TCP/IPv4 settings to be able to join it to your NT domain.

Note: you will need the assistance of your network administrator to provide you by the below required settings.

2-2 Windows Network Configuration

Open Network and Sharing Center from Control Panel --
☐ Network and Internet --☐ Network and Sharing Center

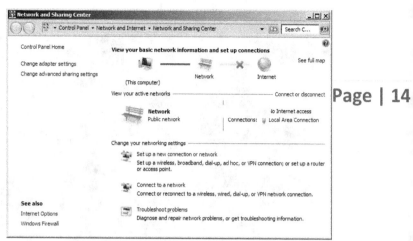

Figure 2-12: Network and Sharing Center

Click on Local Area Connection

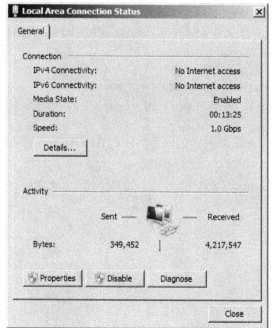

Figure 2-13: Local Area Connection Status

Click on Properties

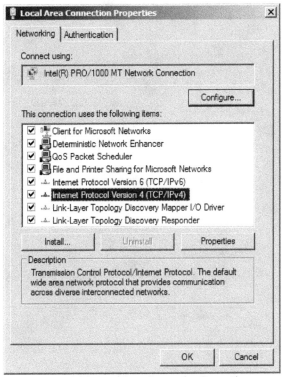

Figure 2-14: Local Area Connection Properties

Click on Internet Protocol Version 4 (TCP/IPv4) then
click Properties

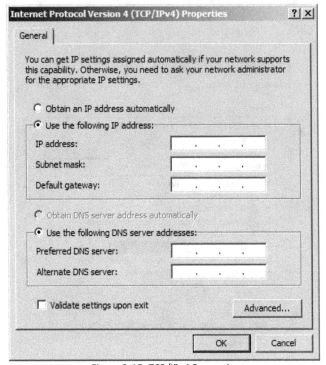

Figure 2-15: TCP/IPv4 Properties

Click on use the following IP address and fill the IP address, Subnet mask and Default gateway fields. Then fill the Preferred and Alternate DNS fields. Then Click OK for all open windows.

2-3 Join Windows Server to NT Domain Step-by-Step

Now you are ready to join the new server to your NT domain.

Note:

You will need your Network Administrator assistance to provide you by the necessary permissions to be able to do the below steps:

1- Right Click on My Computer and click Properties

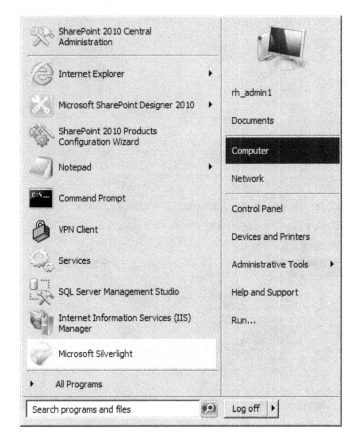

Figure 2-16: Windows Start Menu

Click on Advanced system settings link on the left hand

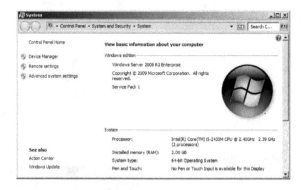

Figure 2-17: System

Click on the computer name tap then click change button, type the computer name and Domain name then click OK

Computer Name/Domain Changes

You can change the name and the membership of this computer. Changes might affect access to network resources. More information

Computer name:

Full computer name:

More...

Member of

○ Domain:

○ Workgroup:

OK   Cancel

Figure 2-18: Computer name/Domain Changes

Provide the required domain credentials that have permission to join the server to your NT domain then restart the server and Login using Domain username and password have administrative privilege on your server.

Chapter3: SQL Server 2008 R2 Deployment

To start installing SQL Server 2008 R2, click on the Setup file inside the License Disk.

The Setup wizard will check the prerequisites needed to be installed, click Ok on the below message to continue.

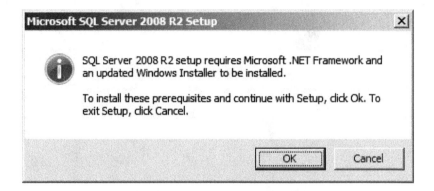

Figure 3-1: Prerequisites needed to be installed

After pressing OK setup wizard will start loading the installation components

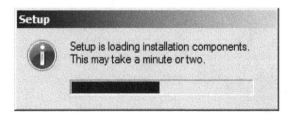

Figure 3-2: Setup loading

The .NET Framework 3.5 SP1 is required; its installation wizard will be launched.

To continue with this wizard, read the License Agreement and choose I have read and <u>A</u>ccept the terms of the License Agreement and click the Install button.

Figure 3-3: .NET Framework 3.5 SP1 download

Now the download and installation window progress will appear.

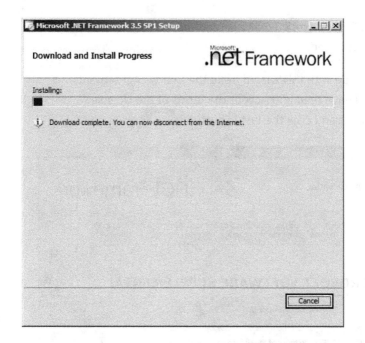

Figure 3-4: .NET Framework 3.5 SP1 setup progress

After the installation completed click exit.

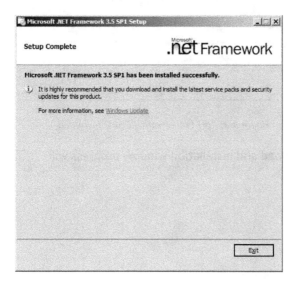

Figure 3-5: .NET Framework 3.5 SP1 setup completion

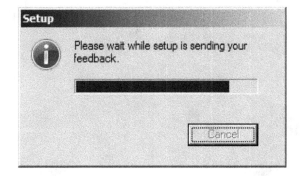

Figure 3-6: Setup sending your feedback to Microsoft

There will be a hot fix will be required to installed, click Ok to start its download and installation wizard.

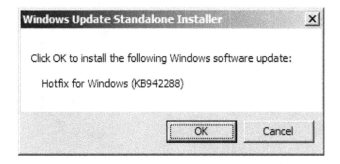

Figure 3-7: Windows update required

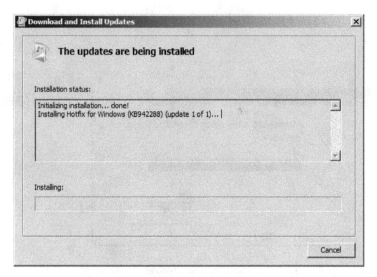

Figure 3-8: Windows update installation

After the installation completed click on Restart Now to restart your server.

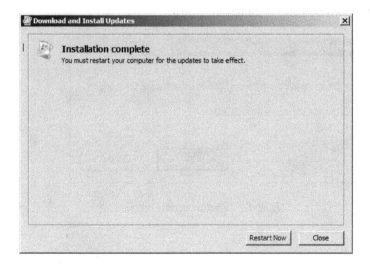

Figure 3-9: Windows update installation completion

In the SQL Server Installation center will appear after clicking again on the Setup file.

Click on the Installation link on the right hand of the window, and click on the New Installation or add features to an existing installation option on the left hand.

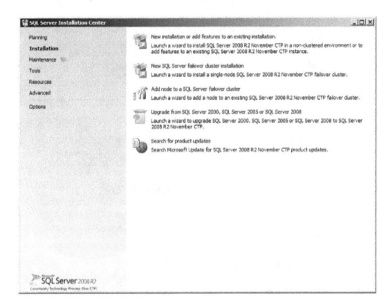

Figure 3-10: SQL Server Installation Center

The Setup Support Rules wizard will check on the required rules, any error will be found should be corrected before starting the installation.

Click Ok to start the installation journey.

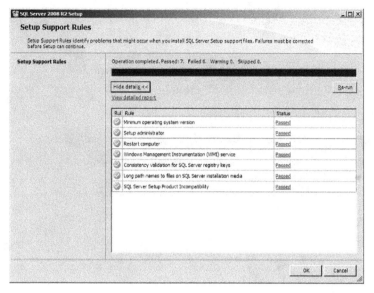

Figure 3-11: SQL Server Setup Support Rules

Specify your licensed edition and type your key.

Figure 3-12: SQL Server Product Key

Accept the License terms after reading them, and then click next

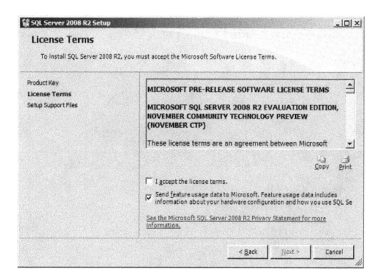

Figure 3-13: SQL Server License Agreement

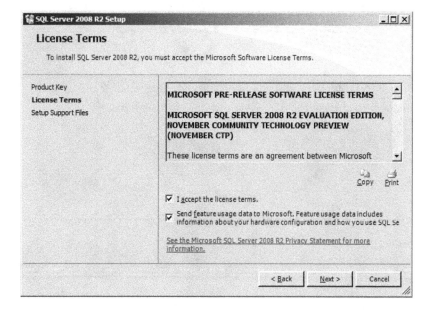

Figure 3-14: SQL Server License terms

Click Install to Setup the required support files.

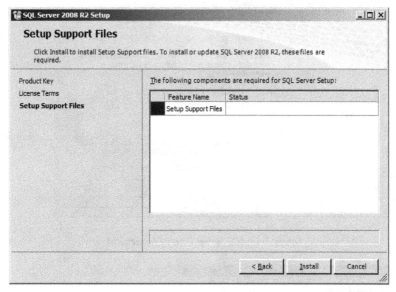

Figure 3-15: SQL Server Setup Support Rules

Choose the role, here you will need the Database Engine Services, so choose the SQL Server feature installation

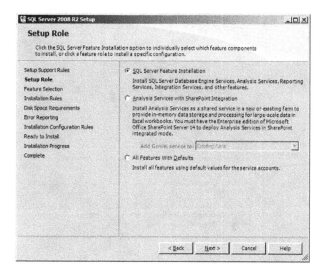

Figure 3-16: SQL Server Setup Role

Now choose the features that you need to be installed then click next.

Note that; don't install the services that won't need to save your server resources like Analysis Service or Reporting Service. Or install them if needed in the future.

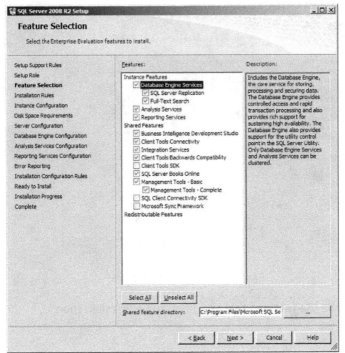

Figure 3-17: SQL Server Feature Selection

The installation wizard will check if the installation process won't face any difficulties during the setup journey. After the check completed click next.

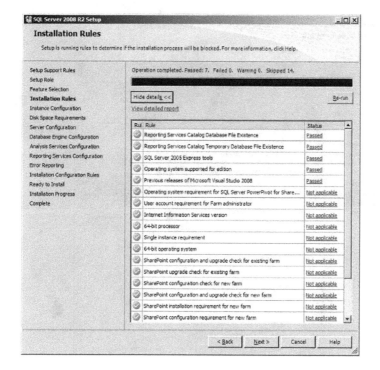

Figure 3-18: SQL Server Installation Rules

In the instance configuration choose the Default Instance and click next

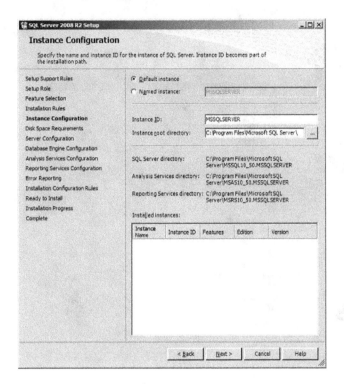

Figure 3-19: SQL Server Instance Configuration

The Setup wizard will check the required free space on Server's hard drive which is required for the features we have selected in the previous steps and click next.

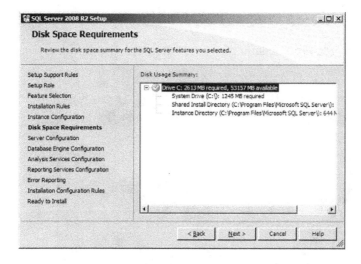

Figure 3-20: SQL Server Disk Space Requirements

Now choose the service accounts that will have permissions to start the SQL server services

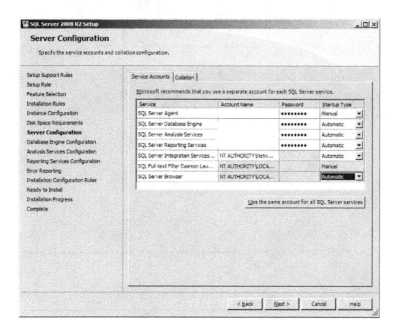

Figure 3-21: SQL Server Configuration- Service Accounts

Choose the required Collation for your Databases Engine, and
then click next

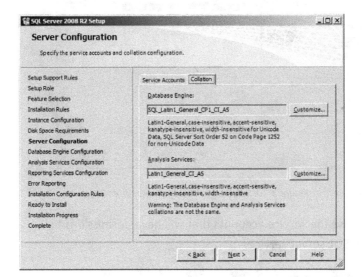

Figure 3-22: SQL Server Configuration – Collation

Choose your Authentication Mode to be mixed, choose the
Domain Account by clicking on Add Current User Button and
type the **sa** password then click next.

Note, keep your sa password in safe place and don't forget it.

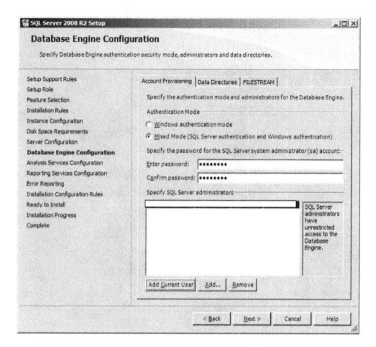

Figure 3-23: Database Engine Configuration- Account Provisioning

Choose the installation Directories and click next.

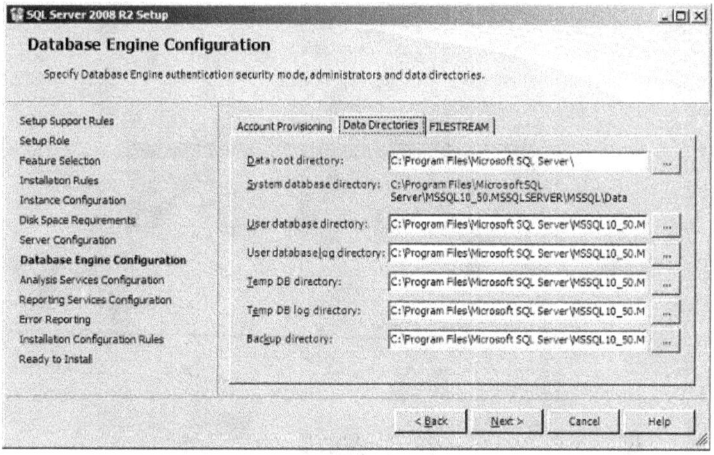

Figure 3-24: Database Engine Configuration- Data Directories

Help Microsoft to improve SQL server features and Services by select the below check box and click next

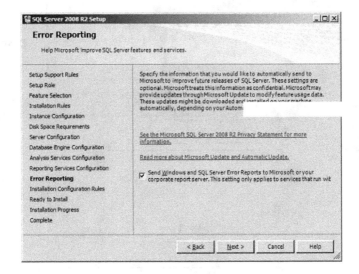

Figure 3-25: Error Reporting

Click next after the Installation Configuration Rules wizard completed

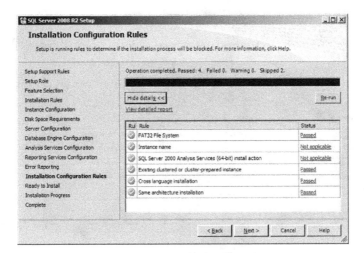

Figure 3-26: Installation Configuration Rules

Review the Summary and Click Install to launch the Installation
Process

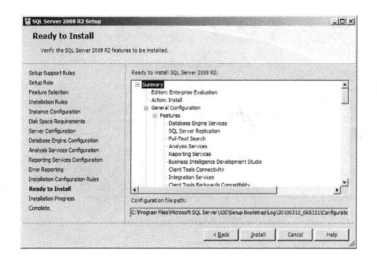

Figure 3-27: Ready to Install

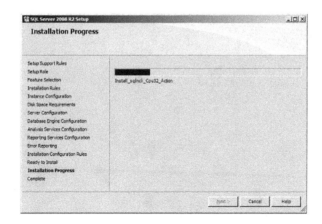

Figure 3-28: Installation Progress

After the Installation Process Completed click close

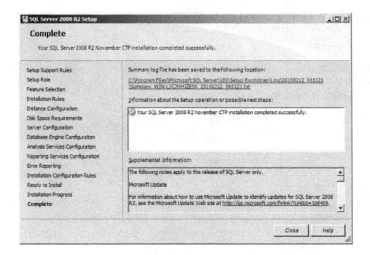

Figure 3-28: Installation completion

Restart the server and go to services to make sure that all SQL server Services are up and running

Chapter4: SharePoint Deployment

4-1 Install SharePoint Prerequisites Automatically

Run PrerequisiteInstaller.exe file from the SharePoint CD source to install the SharePoint prerequisites automatically

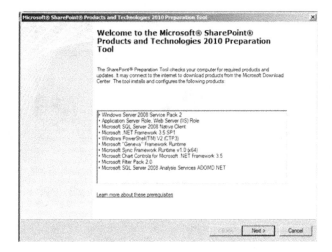

Figure 4-1: SharePoint 2010 Preparation Tool

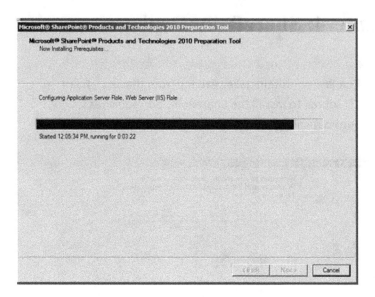

Figure 4-2: SharePoint 2010 Preparation Tool Progress

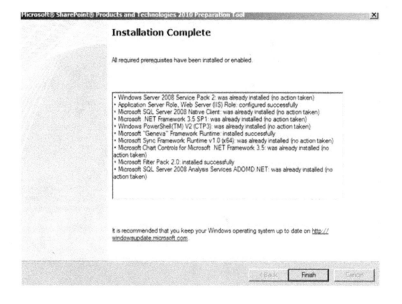

Figure 4-3: SharePoint 2010 Preparation Tool – Installation completion

4-2 Add SharePoint 2010 required Features, Roles and Roles Services Manually

To add Features, Roles and Roles Services manually required by SharePoint 2010:

Check the "Application Server" role and add required features

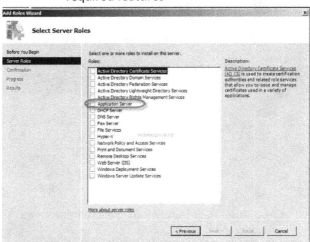

Figure 4-4: Select Server Roles

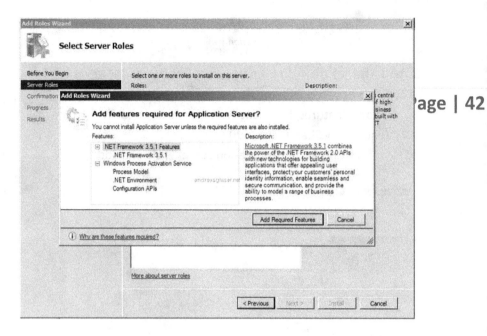

Figure 4-5: Add Roles Wizard

Check the "Web Server (IIS)" role, and proceed
to the feature selection

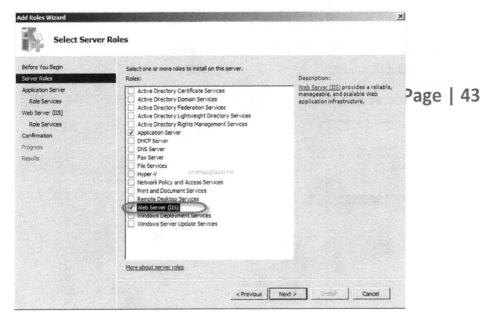

Figure 4-6: Select Server Roles

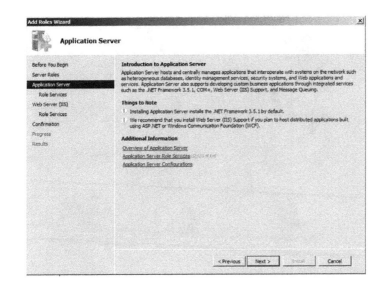

Figure 4-7: Add Roles Wizard

Check all the role services as shown in the picture and add role
services if required.

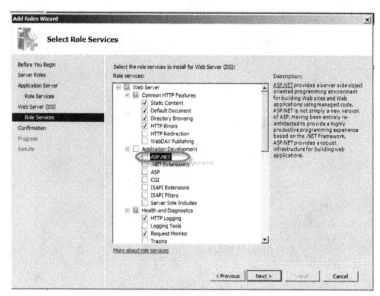

Figure 4-8: Select Role Services

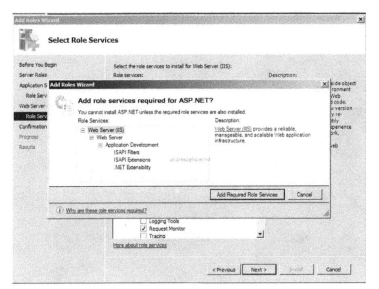

Figure 4-9: Select Role Services

Proceed checking all the role services as shown in the picture.

These role services will be installed by the SharePoint Products and Technologies 2010 Preparation Tool later if you don't do it now.

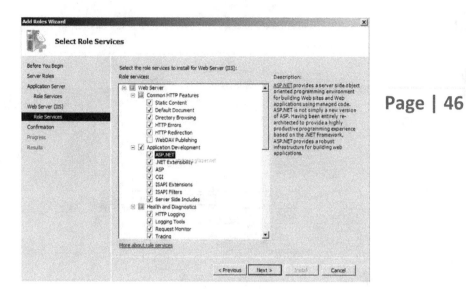

Figure 4-10: Select Role Services

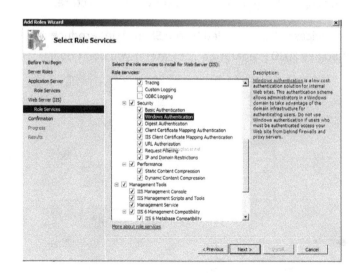

Figure 4-11: Add Roles Wizard

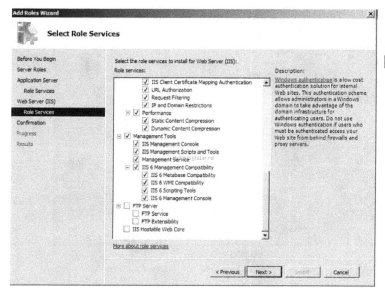

Figure 4-12: Select Role Services

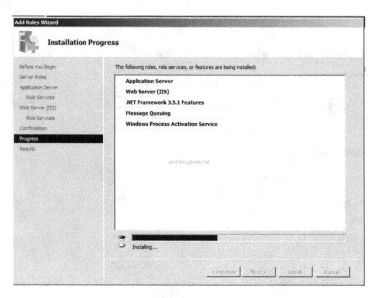

Figure 4-13: Select Role Services- Installation Progress

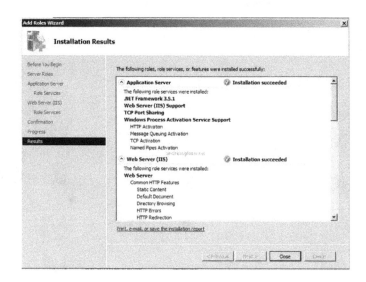

Figure 4-14: Select Role Services- Installation Results

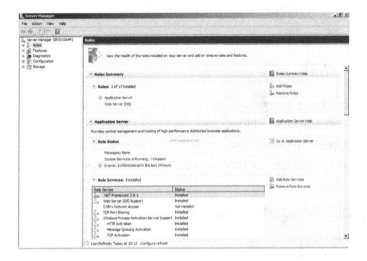

Figure 4-15: Windows 2008 R2 Server Manager

4-3 Install SharePoint 2010 prerequisites manually

To install SharePoint 2010 prerequisites manually, install the below software list:

a. Windows 2008 R2 and Windows Server 2008 KB971831

b. WCF Fix article for Windows 2008 R2 and Windows 7 KB976462

c. Microsoft SQL Server 2008 Native Client

d. Microsoft "Geneva" Framework Runtime

e. Microsoft Sync Framework Runtime v1.0 (x64)

f. Microsoft Chart Controls for Microsoft .NET Framework 3.5

g. Microsoft SQL Server 2008 Analysis Services ADOMD.NET

h. PowerShell V2 RTM

i. SQL Server 2008 SP1

j.　.NET Framework 3.5 Service Pack 1 (Full
Package) KB959209 KB967190

4-4 Start SharePoint 2010 installation

After completing the installation of the prerequisites,
either automatically or manually, click "Install
SharePoint Server" link. SharePoint 2010 Installation
screen prompts for Product Key. TO get beta key Click
here.

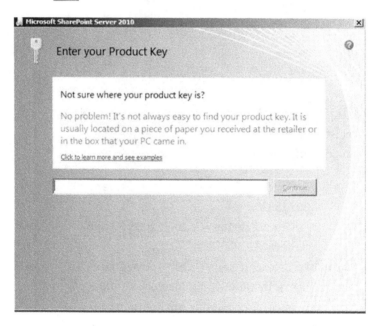

Figure 4-16: SharePoint 2010 Product Key

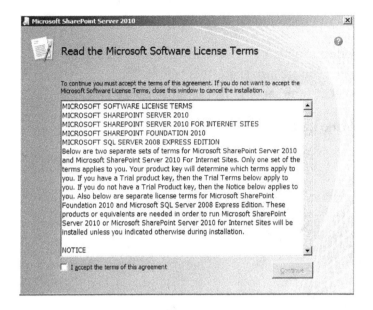

Figure 4-17: Software License Terms

Read your License terms and click I accept and start Installation

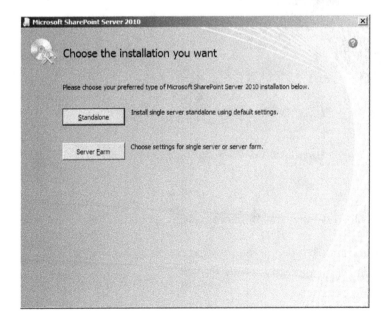

Figure 4-18: SharePoint 2010 Installation Type

Select Standalone option, if you are installing with SQL Express 2008 server. If you are installing SQL Server 2008 and SharePoint 2010 farm servers, then select Server Farm option.

In this scenario the Standalone option will be selected

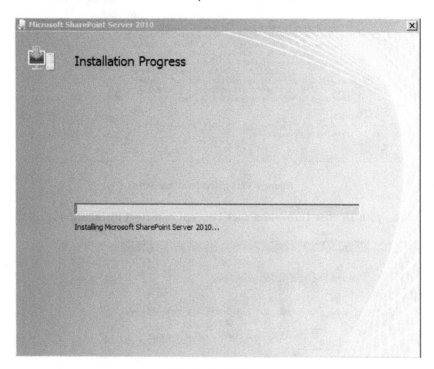

Figure 4-19: SharePoint 2010 Installation Progress

System will start the Installation progress...

System would take several minutes to complete installation and prompt for Configuration Wizard.

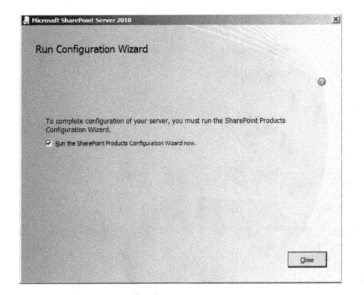

Figure 4-20: SharePoint 2010 Installation Completion

Run your Configuration wizard and click next

Figure 4-21: SharePoint 2010 Configuration Wizard

On Configuration wizard click "Yes" to start IIS and SharePoint Admin, Timer service

Figure 4-22: SharePoint 2010 Configuration Wizard

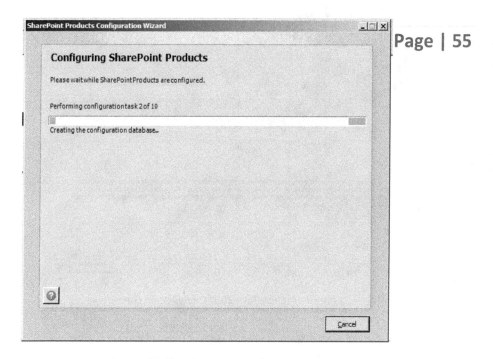

Figure 4-23: SharePoint 2010 Configuration Wizard

Configuration wizard continue 2 of 10 tasks and if everything is ok, the system will display the following screen. (Please note that it will take several minutes to complete. It's not as fast as SharePoint 2007 configuration wizard).

If you got the below message click finish and got to SharePoint 2010 Central Administration

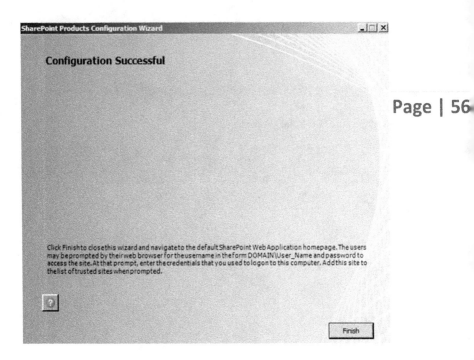

Figure 4-24: SharePoint 2010 Configuration Completion

Chapter5: Troubleshooting

1- If it gives the below error "The application has failed to start because its side-by-side configuration is incorrect. Please see the application event log or use the command-line sxstrace.exe too for more detail". Cope the PrerequisiteInstaller.exe file to local folder called SharePointPrerequisites and run it.

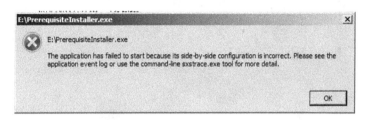

Figure 5-1: SharePoint PrerequisiteInstaller.exe error

2- If you got the below error do the following steps

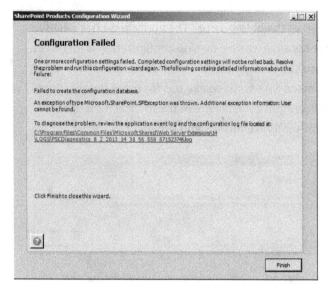

Figure 5-2: SharePoint Configuration Wizard error

    a. Grant the "Network Service" account the full access to the "14" directory under %commonprogramfiles\Microsoft Shared\Web Server Extensions.

    b. Delete the registry key located under "SOFTWARE\Microsoft\Shared Tools\Web Server Extensions\14.0\Secure\FarmAdmin" Registry key and then run the SharePoint 2010 Products Configuration Wizard.

    c. It is likely that this registry key is required to be cleared each time you run the wizard after an unsuccessful attempt

    d. Make sure that your OS is up to date

Re-run the configuration wizard again

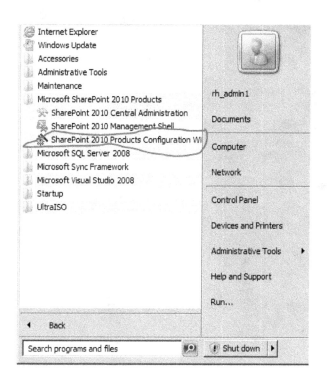

Figure 5-3: SharePoint Configuration Wizard

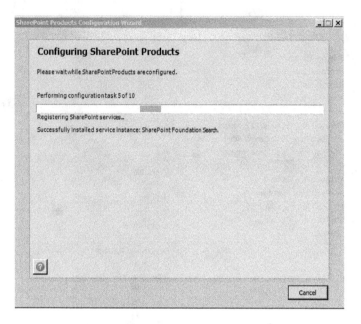

Figure 5-4: SharePoint Configuration Wizard Progress

3- If you got the below error stop windows firewall

Figure 5-5: SharePoint Configuration Wizard error

4- If you got the below error stop windows firewall

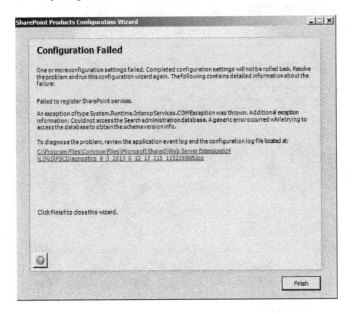

Figure 5-6: SharePoint Configuration Wizard error

5- If you got the below error you can ignore it and go directly to SharePoint 2010 Central Administration

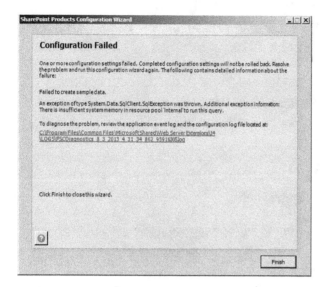

Figure 5-7: SharePoint Configuration Wizard error

References

Install SharePoint 2010:

http://sharepoint-tutorial.net/post/2009/11/17/installing-sharepoint-server-2010-on-windows-server-2008-r2-and-sql-server-2008-r2-part-3-windows-server-2008-r2-configuration.aspx

Download all SharePoint 2010 prerequisites on one-click using PowerShell:

http://blogs.technet.com/b/meacoex/archive/2011/08/07/download-all-sharepoint-2010-prerequisites-on-one-click-using-powershell.aspx

Running the prerequisite installer without an internet connection:

https://www.nothingbutsharepoint.com/sites/devwiki/SP2010Admin/Pages/Running%20the%20prerequisite%20installer%20without%20an%20internet%20connection.aspx

SharePoint prerequisites, this is how you do it!:

http://blog.blksthl.com/2011/10/18/sharepoint-prerequisites-this-is-how-you-do-it/

Step by Step SharePoint Server 2010 Installation Guide

http://www.codeproject.com/Articles/44219/Step-by-Step-SharePoint-Server-2010-Installation-G

Failed to create configuration database on SharePoint 2010 beta install under Windows 7:

http://social.technet.microsoft.com/Forums/sharepoint/en-US/185c1b0f-9cb1-460d-8cd7-c3454314cb7b/failed-to-create-configuration-database-on-sharepoint-2010-beta-install-under-windows-7

SharePoint 2010 Products configuration wizard Errors & Fix

http://sharepointorange.blogspot.com/2012/02/sharepoint-2010-products-configuration.html

SQL Server Installation (SQL Server 2008 R2)

http://msdn.microsoft.com/en-us/library/bb500469(SQL.105).aspx

How to install SQL Server 2008 R2

http://www.sqlcoffee.com/SQLServer2008_0013.htm

Configure TCP/IP settings

http://technet.microsoft.com/en-us/library/cc731673(v=ws.10).aspx